SHORT WALKS

MADE EASY

PEAK DIS

Contents

Walk 1

HOLME AND FOUR RESERVOIRS

Distance
3.2 miles / 5.1km

Time
2 hours   CATCH A BUS

Start/Finish
Ramsden Reservoir

Parking HD9 2QW
Ramsden car park,
Brownhill Lane

Cafés / pubs
The Fleece Inn, Holme

Scenic Holme valley, with moors, woods and reservoirs

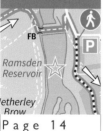

FB

Ramsden
Reservoir

etherley
Brow

Page 14

Walk 2

LANGSETT RESERVOIR

Distance
3.6 miles/5.8km

Time
2 hours

CATCH A BUS

Start/Finish
Langsett Barn

Parking S36 4GY
Langsett Barn
car park, off A616

Cafés/pubs
Waggon and Horses;
Bank View Café

Attractive circuit
of large reservoir
with wartime
history

Walk 3

CASTLETON

Distance
4.1 miles/6.6km

Time
2¾ hours

CATCH A BUS

Start/Finish
Castleton

Parking S33 8WN
Long-stay car
park, Castleton

Cafés/pubs
Castleton

Peak Cavern
show cave, lead
mines and Mam
Tor views

Walk 4

LONGSHAW AND BURBAGE BRIDGE

Distance
3.6 miles/5.8km

Time
2 hours

CATCH A BUS

Start/Finish
Longshaw Estate

Parking S11 7TY
NT Woodcroft car
park, off A6187

Cafés/pubs
NT café; Fox House
Inn nearby

Parkland and
moorland, pack-
horse bridge and
Toad's Mouth Rock

Walk 5

MACCLESFIELD CANAL AND RAILWAY

Distance
2.8 miles/4.5km

Time
1¼ hours CATCH A BUS

Start/Finish
Nelson Pit car park

Parking SK12 1TH
Nelson Pit car park

Cafés/pubs
Higher Poynton and Adlington

Coal mining and railway heritage and colourful canal towpath

Page 42

Walk 6

TEGG'S NOSE

Distance
2.7 miles/4.3km

Time
1¾ hours

Start/Finish
Tegg's Nose Car Park

Parking SK11 0AP
Tegg's Nose Country Park car park

Cafés/pubs
Country Park café; pub in Langley

Superlative view-point, quarrying heritage and silk manufacture

Page 48

Walk 7

MONSAL TRAIL AND CHEE DALE

Distance
4.3 miles/6.9km

Time
2½ hours CATCH A BUS

Start/Finish
Millers Dale

Parking SK17 8SN
Millers Dale car park, off B6049

Cafés/pubs
Café at start; pub in Millers Dale village

Exhilarating scenery and rich flora, stepping stones through gorge

Page 54

Walk 8	Walk 9	Walk 10

BUXTON COUNTRY PARK

MANIFOLD WAY

ILAM

Distance
1.4 miles/2.3km

Distance
3.2 miles/5.2km

Distance
1.9 miles/3km

Time
1 hour
GO BY TRAIN CATCH A BUS

Time
1¾ hours
CATCH A BUS

Time
1 hour

Start/Finish
Poole's Cavern, Buxton

Start/Finish
Hulme End

Start/Finish
Ilam Hall

Parking SK17 9BB
Poole's Cavern car park

Parking SK17 0HF
National Park Centre
car park

Parking DE6 2AZ
National Trust
car park

Cafés/pubs
Café at the Cavern

Cafés/pubs
Tea Junction café;
Manifold Inn, Hulme End

Cafés/pubs
National Trust
tearoom, Ilam Hall

**Poole's Cavern;
winding woodland
and hillside paths
to viewpoint folly**

**Classic level walk:
cliffs, meandering
river meadows
and woods**

**Superb parkland
stroll around
former monastic
and country estate**

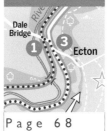

GETTING OUTSIDE
IN THE PEAK DISTRICT

"

the valley floor
is so constricted
the path takes
to a line of large
stepping stones
embedded into
the river – how
fantastic is that!

OS Champion
Yvonne Witter

Tegg's Nose Reservoir

A very warm welcome to the new Short Walks Made Easy guide to the Peak District – what a fantastic selection of leisurely walks we have for you!

Located at the southern end of the Pennines, with neighbouring Greater Manchester to the west and Sheffield to the east, it is unsurprising that the glorious countryside of the Peak District makes this national park one of the most visited in Great Britain.

These walks encapsulate a variety of enticing landscapes ripe for exploring. The underlying rock of the northern half of the national park is gritstone, giving rise to the 'Dark Peak' – an area characterized by rolling heather moorland, such as the *Last of the Summer Wine* country around Holme, and long-abandoned quarrying on the dramatically weather-worn cliffs (known as 'edges') and visible on the route to Tegg's Nose, a superlative viewpoint. In its southern half, the gritstone gives way to limestone, and the grassy plateau of the 'White Peak', typified by the Derbyshire Dales, is partitioned by drystone walls and deeply incised by pretty, meandering gorges as explored in the Manifold valley and Chee Dale. Here the valley floor is so constricted the path takes to a line of large stepping stones embedded into the river – how fantastic is that!

There's an attractive parkland walk around the historic country estate of Ilam; famous show caves can be visited on the Castleton and Buxton rambles; while easy-going strolls can be enjoyed beside the colourful Macclesfield Canal and along the Monsal Trail, a former railway trackbed.

Yvonne Witter, OS Champion

WE SMILE MORE
WHEN WE'RE OUTSIDE

Cave Dale

Whether it's a short walk during our lunch break or a full day's outdoor adventure, we know that a good dose of fresh air is just the tonic we all need.

At Ordnance Survey (OS), we're passionate about helping more people to get outside more often. It sits at the heart of everything we do, and through our products and services, we aim to help you lead an active outdoor lifestyle, so that you can live longer, stay younger and enjoy life more.

We firmly believe the outdoors is for everyone, and we want to help you find the very best Great Britain has to offer. We are blessed with an island that is beautiful and unique, with a rich and varied landscape. There are coastal paths to meander along, woodlands to explore, countryside to roam, and cities to uncover. Our trusted source of inspirational content is bursting with ideas for places to go, things to do and easy beginner's guides on how to get started.

It can be daunting when you're new to something, so we want to bring you the know-how from the people who live and breathe the outdoors. To help guide us, our team of awe-inspiring OS Champions share their favourite places to visit, hints and tips for outdoor adventures, as well as tried and tested accessible, family and wheelchair-friendly routes. We hope that you will feel inspired to spend more time outside and reap the physical and mental health benefits that the outdoors has to offer. With our handy guides, paper and digital mapping, and exciting new apps, we can be with you every step of the way.

To find out more visit os.uk/getoutside

RESPECTING
THE COUNTRYSIDE

You can't beat getting outside in the British countryside, but it's vital that we leave no trace when we're enjoying the great outdoors.

Let's make sure that generations to come can enjoy the countryside just as we do.

Leave no trace

Keep dogs under control; bin and bag waste

Do not light fires; only BBQ at official sites

Leave gates as you find them

Keep to footpaths and open access land

Plan ahead for your trip

For more details please visit
www.gov.uk/countryside-code

USING THIS GUIDE

Easy-to-follow Peak District walks for all

Before setting off
Check the walk information panel to plan your outing

- Consider using **Public transport** where flagged. If driving, note the satnav postcode for the car park under **Parking**

- The suggested **Time** is based on a gentle pace

- Note the availability of **Cafés**, tearooms and pubs, and **Toilets**

Terrain and hilliness

- **Terrain** indicates the nature of the route surface

- Any rises and falls are noted under **Hilliness**

Walking with your dog?

- This panel states where **Dogs** must be on a lead and how many stiles there are – in case you need to lift your dog

- Keep dogs on leads where there are livestock and between April and August on moorland where there are ground-nesting birds

A perfectly pocket-sized walking guide

- Handily sized for ease of use on each walk

- When not being read, it fits nicely into a pocket...

- ...so between points, put this book in the pocket of your coat, trousers or day sack and enjoy your stroll in glorious national park countryside – we've made it pocket-sized for a reason!

Flexibility of route presentation to suit all readers

- **Not comfortable map reading?** Then use the simple-to-follow route profile and accompanying route description and pictures

- **Happy to map read?** New-look walk mapping makes it easier for you to focus on the route and the points of interest along the way

- **Read the insightful Did you know?, Local legend, Stories behind the walk** and **Nature notes** to help you make the most of your day out and to enjoy all that each walk has to offer

The easy-to-use walk map

- **Large-scale** mapping for ultra-clear route finding

- **Numbered points** at key turns along the route that tie in with the route instructions and respective points marked on the profile

- **Pictorial symbols** for intuitive map reading, see Map Symbols on the front cover flap

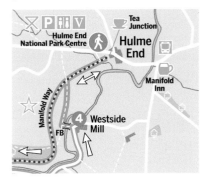

The simple-to-follow walk profile

- Progress easily along the route using the illustrative profile, it has **numbered points** for key turning points and **graduated distance** markers

- Easy-read **route directions** with turn-by-turn detail

- Reassuring **route photographs** for each numbered point

Many of the features and symbols shown are taken from Ordnance Survey's celebrated **Explorer** mapping, designed to help people across Great Britain enjoy leisure time spent outside. For more on this – and how you can start planning your own walks and adventures, please see the inside back cover.

HOLME AND FOUR RESERVOIRS

The wild moors and countryside around the Holme valley featured widely in the long-running TV series *Last of the Summer Wine*. Nora Batty's house, Sid's Café and a fascinating museum are just a short ride away in Holmfirth, but first try this lovely walk past the four Ramsden reservoirs. Glorious woodland and splendid views along the valleys to the high moors are characteristic features of the route, while there is a welcoming pub in Holme.

Distance	3.2 miles/5.1km
Time	2 hours
Start/Finish	Ramsden Reservoir
Parking	HD9 2QW Ramsden car park, Brownhill Lane
Public toilets	Holme, opposite The Fleece Inn
Cafés/pubs	The Fleece Inn, Holme
Terrain	Forest tracks, woodland and field paths
Hilliness	Gentle climbs on forest tracks; steep stepped descent after ❺ to Gill Hey Bridge; descent and climb after ❼
Footwear	Year round

Public transport

Bus services to Holme (an alternative start point), www.traveline.info

 Accessibility

Pushchairs on water authority access drive/forest road to **2**. Track is rough/pot-holed so may not suit all wheelchairs

 Dogs

Welcome but on leads. Five stiles

Did you know? The upland moors were once covered in forest. Clearance began with the introduction of farming during the Bronze Age (5,000 to 3,500 years ago), continuing steadily through the centuries as land was turned to agriculture and pasture, leaving woodland only on the steep-sided cloughs (valleys). Most of today's forests surrounding the reservoirs are relatively recent plantings to reduce erosion and improve water quality as well as to provide a cash crop.

Local legend Ramsden Clough at the head of the valley above Riding Wood Reservoir was once known locally as Monkey Nick, after a man walking his dog there in 1852 came across a monkey. It was thought to have escaped from a travelling circus, where it rode around the ring on horseback to the delight of the audience.

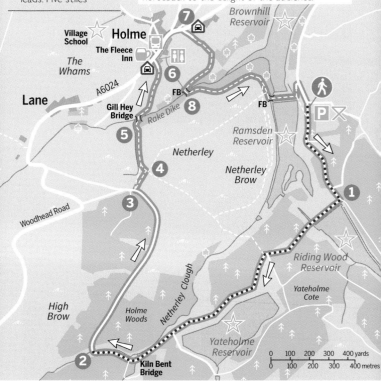

STORIES BEHIND THE WALK

☆ **Water-powered Industry** The first factories processing wool and cotton were powered by water and many mills sprang up along the Holme valley to take advantage of its fast-flowing river. But summer droughts and winter ice could stop the machinery and small reservoirs were built to help regulate the supply and maintain production. However, these were not without their problems; the collapse of the nearby Bilberry Dam in 1852 devastated the valley, killing 81 people.

☆ **Ramsden Valley Reservoirs** Today, four dams occupy the Ramsden valley above Holmbridge. The highest and oldest, Yateholme, was opened in 1879 to supply the expanding populations and industry of West Yorkshire, and is somewhat unusual in that it occupies the valley side rather than the base of Netherley Clough, necessitating a long, three-sided embankment. It is seen over to the right as you climb from Netherley Clough. The lowest reservoir, Brownhill, is the most recent. It opened in 1932 and holds more water than the other three put together.

Riding Wood Reservoir ☆

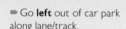

1 ½ mile

➡ Go **left** out of car park along lane/track.
➡ After ¼ mile, keep past cottages then swing **right** onto dam of Riding Wood Reservoir.

1 ➡ Keep with ongoing track.
➡ Follow it to meet the high grassy bank holding back Yateholme Reservoir.
➡ Bend **right** with track beneath bank; in ½ mile reach sharp **right**-hand bend in track across Netherley Clough.

☆ Broadcasting

Perched on the hill above the valley is the Holme Moss Transmitter, which began broadcasting BBC TV in 1951 with VHF radio following in 1956. The present mast, put up in 1985, is one of the highest and most powerful VHF transmitters in the country. Glimpsed later in the walk to the north-east is Emley Moor Transmitter; at 1,084 feet it is the largest freestanding tower in Britain. It replaces an earlier mast, which collapsed under the weight of ice and wind in 1969.

☆ Village School

The village school in Holme was one of the earliest in the valley and was endowed in 1693 by one Joshua Earnshaw. Standing on the corner of Field Head Lane it was rebuilt by public subscription in 1838 and later extended with an upper floor, accommodating both day and Sunday schools. Following the 1870 Education Act a new Board School was built on what is now Meal Hill Road, and it continues to serve the community today.

Yateholme
☆ Reservoir

1 mile

1½ miles

2 ➡ Walk with rising track beside forest for a little over ½ mile to signed stile in wall on **right**.

3 ➡ Climb stile and head down by fence to find a stile on right.

NATURE NOTES

The trees and open moors are home to many birds, although they are more likely to be heard than seen. Listen for the cascading musical song of skylarks, the haunting call of curlew or the lapwing, often dubbed a 'peewit', which describes its cry. On the water you might see black-headed gulls, Canada geese or even a cormorant.

Cormorant

Black-headed gull

The Fleece Inn

2 miles

Gill Hey Bridge

4
➡ Ignore this stile. Instead swing **left** to walk away by curving broken wall, keeping it on your left.
➡ It leads down to stile at the bottom of a rough field.

5
➡ Cross into wood and follow stone steps steeply down to Gill Hey Bridge.
➡ Over bridge, climb **right**, shortly passing through gate and on to second gate into cottage garden.

6
➡ Follow garden edge, leaving through gate at top onto road, opposite The Fleece.
➡ Turn **right** through village. Bear **right** past small square; bear **right** again at fork (left goes to Digley Reservoir).
➡ In 50 yards find path signed **right**.

Moss and wood sorrel in Rake Dike Clough

Canada goose

Lapwing

Brownhill Reservoir ☆ Ramsden ☆ Reservoir

2½ miles **8** 3 miles

8 ▪ On far bank, climb **left**. Stick with ongoing path curving above Brownhill Reservoir.
▪ Head down into trees then swing **left** below Ramsden Reservoir dam.
▪ Join climbing track at far side and cross spillway up to lane. Turn **right** back to car park.

7 ▪ Follow path through gate and over stile into a field.
▪ Slant down to another stile in bottom corner; follow ongoing path through trees to footbridge over Rake Dike.

WALK 2

LANGSETT
RESERVOIR

Langsett Reservoir is a popular local
beauty spot and this scenic walk
combines the lakeside plantation
and woods with a return across the
moorland flanks of Hingcliff Common.
After passing the lonely ruin of North
America Farm, the final stretch follows
a lane across the Langsett Dam, which
towers impressively over the valley
below.

Distance	3.6 miles/5.8km
Time	2 hours
Start/Finish	Langsett Barn
Parking S36 4GY	Langsett Barn car park, off A616, just west of Langsett
Public toilets	Langsett Barn
Cafés/pubs	Waggon and Horses and Bank View Café at start
Terrain	Woodland and moorland paths; some lane
Hilliness	Descent into wood after start; steady climb onto moor after ❷

Did you know? Langsett Reservoir is over a mile long, covers 121 acres and has a capacity of around 1,400 million gallons of water. However, although it might look inviting on a hot summer's day, it is definitely not for swimming in!

Local legend The old name for the area was Lang Side, or Long Slope, up which livestock were driven to the higher summer pastures having been wintered in the shelter of the valley.

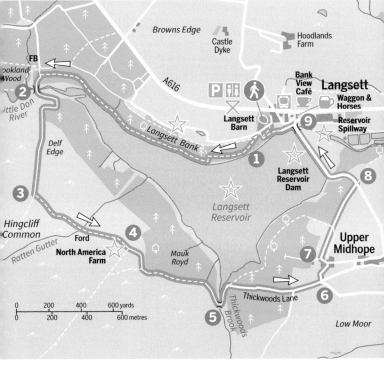

STORIES BEHIND THE WALK

☆**Water for the Towns** Like many others in the area, Langsett Reservoir was a direct product of the Industrial Revolution. Vast numbers of people had migrated to the growing towns to work in new factories and mills and the provision of clean water to replace inadequate and often polluted local wells and springs became a public health necessity, particularly in the overcrowded slums of late Victorian Britain. The reservoir here was completed in 1904 to provide water for Sheffield and Barnsley.

☆**An Ambitious Project** The reservoir's construction took six years and a small town sprang up to house around 170 navvies and their families. The buildings were of corrugated iron and included a mission, small hospital, recreation reading rooms and a school. The dam itself is one of the largest earth embankments in the country and the project included an elaborate valve house and residence for the dam keeper, both built in a baronial Gothic style.

Waggon and Horses ☕☕ Bank View Café ☆ Langsett Reservoir ☆ Langsett Bank

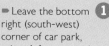

¦ ½ mile

➤ Leave the bottom right (south-west) corner of car park, taking **left**-most path ahead.
➤ Bear **left** again at an immediate fork and continue down to join another path.

1 ➤ Follow it **right**, above the lake, keeping **left** at successive junctions.
➤ Eventually meet a stone-paved track, which leads down to bridge across the Little Don River.

2 ➤ Cross and keep **left**, winding uphill beyond the trees onto open moor.
➤ Ascend for ½ mile to fork.

☆ **Wartime Langsett** During World War II, the area around the reservoirs was used for military training and artillery practice as well as housing troops to protect the dams. The concrete track followed as you approach ❻ was one of several built to take tanks, while the abandoned North America Farm was used for gunnery practice. After the Dambuster Raids in 1943, a high steel wire curtain was erected to prevent low-flying bombers from reaching the dam, which if breached would have caused untold damage and loss of life along the valley.

☆ **Depopulating the Moor** To ensure the purity of the water, six small farms that previously dotted the hillside of the catchment area were cleared. Among these was North America Farm, whose ruins still stand beside the moorland path. The land is now largely heather moor, which is managed for the benefit of wildlife, in particular, red grouse. Patches of old heather are regularly burned to encourage new growth on which the birds feed.

Hingcliff Common

❸ 1½ miles

❷ 1 mile

❺ ▪ On far bank, swing **left** with track, rising to gate.
▪ Keep with main track; later go through another gate and along concrete track past barrier onto lane corner.

❹ ▪ Keep with ongoing track through gate, soon descending towards trees.
▪ Eventually drop to bridge over Thickwoods Brook.

❸ ▪ Bear **left** for another ¼ mile to reach ruin of North America Farm.

Walk 2 Langsett Reservoir **23**

NATURE NOTES

On the open moor, sphagnum moss is a small plant that grows closely together on wet ground and can form large sponge-like hummocks. Cotton grass, often seen in carpeting swathes, is unmistakeable in early summer. The white, fluffy seed-heads were once used for candlewicks, but the wary walker will steer clear, for they often mark waterlogged ground.

Management of moorlands to support red grouse shooting also helps many other birds, including golden plover. Other species include hunters such as buzzard, sparrowhawk and short-eared owl.

Red grouse

Cotton grass

☆ **North America Farm**

4

2 miles

5
Thickwoods Brook 2½ miles

6 ➡ Turn immediately **left** on rising bridleway to Upper Midhope.
➡ At the top, go **left** past cottages; in front of gate, follow footpath signed **right**.

7 ➡ Keep **ahead** as path merges with track; continue to meet lane.

Short-eared owl

Golden plover

Sphagnum moss

Upper Midhope
7
3 miles

Langsett
Reservoir dam
8

Reservoir spillway
9
3½ miles

Waggon and Horses

Bank View Café

8 ➤ Go **left**; follow road across Langsett Reservoir dam.
➤ Cross spillway at far side then look for signed path **left** below Manager's house.

9 ➤ Walk beside spillway, rising to junction.
➤ Turn sharp **right**, climbing short flight of steps back to car park.

This page (clockwise): Ramsden Reservoir from Riding Wood; Little Don River, near Langsett; Saxon cross, Ilam; Packhorse bridge, Longshaw Opposite (clockwise): Looking towards Peveril Castle, Castleton; River Manifold; Peak and Northern Footpaths Society sign, Langsett

PEAK & NORTHERN
FOOTPATHS SOCIETY

Nº 51   2000
(1924)

PUBLIC FOOTPATH

AND BRIDLE ROAD VIA
CUT GATE & SLIPPERY STONES
TO DERWENT AND ASHOP VALLEY
FLOUCH INN AND HAZLEHEAD →
← PLEASE KEEP DOGS ON LEADS
LEAVE NO LITTER

27

CATCH A BUS

CASTLETON

One of the most popular Peak District centres, Castleton is famous for its caves, a castle and festivals throughout the year. It is also a great place for exploring the outdoors and the national park centre by the car park has informative displays highlighting the area's history and things to look for. This walk climbs through Cave Dale beneath the castle to the hill above, where the scale of the town's lead-mining industry can be seen. It returns to the town past the Peak Cavern show cave.

Distance	4.1 miles/6.6km (Alternative route 3 miles/4.8km)
Time	2¾ hours
Start/Finish	Castleton
Parking S33 8WN	Long-stay car park, Castleton
Public toilets	In car park
Cafés/pubs	Castleton
Terrain	Hill paths and tracks, some rougher ground
Hilliness	Steady climb through Cave Dale and hillside descent back to Castleton

Did you know? The castle is claimed to be one of the oldest Norman fortresses in England. It was founded by William Peveril shortly after the Norman invasion in 1066 to control the area's lead- and silver-mining industries and to administer the High Peak Royal Forest on behalf of the king. Although later expanded under Henry II, the castle and its garrison never saw action and fell into disuse during the 16th century.

Local legend The hills around Castleton are the only place in Britain where the semi-precious Blue John stone is found. The blue- and purple-banded fluorite was traditionally held to have been discovered by the Romans while mining for lead, but the earliest references to its use in Britain date only from the middle of the 18th century, when the stone was mined to produce elegant vases and decorative panels. Small quantities are still mined today from the Treak Cliff Cavern.

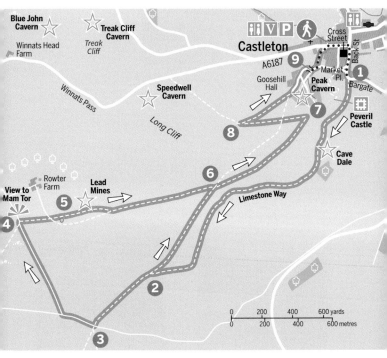

STORIES BEHIND THE WALK

Shivering Mountain Mam Tor, seen across to the left as you return to Castleton, is known as the Shivering Mountain, and incredibly has been subject to an ongoing landslide for the last 4,000 years. The south-eastern face is the most dramatic, where successive slumps have created a massive, unstable cliff falling from the summit. The town's main road from the west once ran across it, but was finally closed to traffic after a landslide in 1979.

☆ **Prehistoric Settlement** The Castleton area has been settled since at least the Bronze Age (2500BC). The highest point is Mam Tor on which an extensive fort was built during the Iron Age (from 800BC). Inside, some 70 hut platforms have been identified, suggesting a sizeable settlement. There is a straightforward, if rather strenuous, ridge walk past it from a car park at the foot of the hill, over Mam Tor and Back Tor to Lose Hill.

 Peveril Castle Cave Dale

½ mile 1 mile

➡ Go **left** out of car park along Cross Street.

➡ At bend, turn **right** up Back Street; keep **left** past Market Place into Bargate.

➡ In a few yards, look for narrow street signed **right** to Cave Dale.

1 ➡ Follow it past cottages, through a gate and gradually climb narrow dale.

➡ After passing through three gates, look for three-way signpost.

☆ **Lead Mines** Lead mining was an important industry in the area, perhaps from Roman times, and it continued into the 19th century. The scars of mining can be seen all across the countryside; long lines of grassed-over humps and hollows remain from countless shallow mines that followed the narrow seams of lead ore across the landscape. By the 19th century, the deposits began to run out and, in the face of cheaper foreign imports, the industry slowly declined.

☆ Caves

Limestone is slightly soluble in rainwater, which seeps into the ground, enlarging cracks and fissures into caves and creating subterranean passages, chambers and watercourses. The area around Castleton is particularly honeycombed; there are numerous small caves as well as four splendid 'show caves' open to the public. Treak Cliff can be seen on the hillside to the north as the route nears the town, while the entrance to Peak Cavern, known as the Devil's Arse, is passed at the end.

---

2   3

1½ miles   2 miles

2 ➡ **For shortcut**, go sharp right at signpost and walk up beside wall. Over hill crest, continue gently down to stile by large sycamore – read on from **6**.
➡ Go past signpost to fork; keep **left** on a broad swathe over hill. Reach a track through gates at far corner.

3 ➡ Immediately go **right** through a gate.
➡ After 200 yards, approaching gate, bend **right** with main trail. Continue 700 yards to another gate.

NATURE NOTES

Cave Dale is a fine example of a dry valley – the result of a fast-flowing glacial stream cutting through the still-frozen hillside at the end of the last glacial period. After the permafrost melted, the water seeped through cracks, dissolving the soluble limestone to create an underground passage. That subsequently collapsed to create a deep gorge. At the foot of the dale, there used to be a natural rock arch, a remnant of the former cave.

Plants to look for during the walk include common rock rose, hart's tongue fern, biting stonecrop, maidenhair spleenwort, mountain pansy and moonwort.

Common rock rose

Hart's tongue fern

View to Mam Tor

④ ⑤ ☆ ¦ 2½ miles

Lead Mines

⑥ ¦

3 miles ¦

④ ➡ Through that, turn immediately **right** over ladder stile signed Castleton.
➡ Walk past walled enclosure (an old pond associated with adjacent mines) to fence stile.

⑤ ➡ The grass path, signed Castleton, continues parallel to old workings for nearly ½ mile, crossing stiles from field to field, eventually reaching stile and gate by a solitary sycamore.

⑥ ➡ Cross and follow ongoing swathe, aiming on the horizon towards top corner of a walled wood concealing the keep of Peveril Castle.

Biting stonecrop

Maidenhair spleenwort

Mountain pansy

Peak Cavern
☆ (right)

3½ miles

4 miles

P
ℹ️
V

7 ➤ About 75 yards before reaching trees, watch for a faint, narrower grass path leaving sharp **left**.
➤ It cuts back across steep hillside to meet wall bend at the bottom.

8 ➤ Turn sharp **right**; walk beside wall, eventually passing through gate at foot of wood.
➤ Past cottages, ongoing track becomes lane, dropping to bridge over stream emanating from Peak Cavern (right) and bear **left**.

9 ➤ Take next **left**, a narrow road that leads out to main street.
➤ Cross to the car park opposite.

LONGSHAW AND BURBAGE BRIDGE

This pleasant walk follows a circular route through the National Trust's Longshaw Estate, wandering through meadows and woodland as well as passing a small lake and lively stream. The day can be extended onto the edge of the open moor, where there is an ancient stone packhorse bridge and fine views to the surrounding hills upon which are old quarries and a prehistoric hillfort.

Distance
3.6 miles / 5.8 km

Time
2 hours

Start/Finish
Longshaw Estate (NT)

Parking S11 7TY
Woodcroft car park, off A6187

Public toilets
NT Visitor Centre, Longshaw Lodge

Cafés/pubs
Café at NT Visitor Centre; Fox House Inn near car park

Terrain
Estate paths and moorland track

Hilliness
Gentle gradients

Footwear
Winter 🥾
Spring/Autumn 🥾👟
Summer 👟

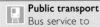

Public transport
Bus service to
Longshaw, www.
traveline.info

Accessibility
Wheelchairs
from car park to
Longshaw Lodge.
Pushchairs on
estate paths from
car park to **3**

Dogs
Welcome but
on leads. One stile

Did you know? The Longshaw Sheepdog Trials
claim to be the oldest, continuously held such
event in the country and, apart from during both
World Wars, have taken place every year since
1898. They proved popular from the start, and
many local hospitals and charities have benefited
from the proceeds.

Local legend Close to Longshaw Lodge are a
couple of springs named for Robin Hood and
Little John. Reputedly, Little John came from
nearby Hathersage, where his supposed grave
can be seen in St Michael's churchyard.

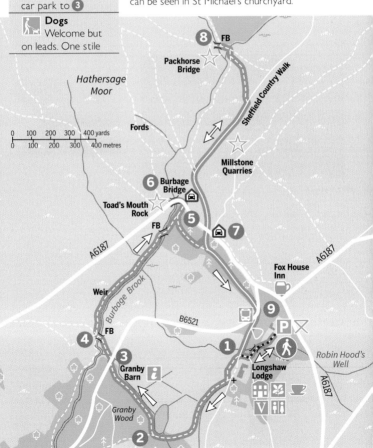

STORIES BEHIND THE WALK

☆ **Pre-industrial Trade Routes** The packhorse bridge dates from the mid-18th century and connected local towns and villages. Long packhorse trains led by 'jaggers' travelled up to 25 miles a day, each animal carrying up to 3cwt (or 336lbs). Loads included salt, coal and wool as well as supplies for local markets. Goods were carried in panniers either side of the beast, hence the bridge has no parapets, so as not to impede progress.

☆ **An Intriguing Boulder** A gigantic, canted, weather-worn boulder overlooking the road beside Burbage Bridge is known as Toad's Mouth Rock. Its shape does indeed resemble the head of a toad, with a natural fissure depicting the mouth and added carvings to represent eyes.

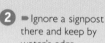

P **✕**

☆ **V** ☆ ☕ ➊

Longshaw Lodge

➼ Leave bottom corner of car park on downhill path leading over a bridge.
➼ At the end, go **right** to junction with main drive by café.

½ mile

➋ Granby Wood

Granby Barn **i**

➌

➊ ➼ Cross to path opposite and follow it **left** past lodge.
➼ Through a gate, bear **right** on path between rhododendrons.
➼ After another gate, continue across park towards Granby Wood and a small lake.

➋ ➼ Ignore a signpost there and keep by water's edge.
➼ Beyond a gate, bear **right** at fork, shortly winding out to road past Granby Barn (information centre).

☆ **Millstone Quarries** To the right of the track onto the moor, the cliffs were quarried for millstones, an industry that dates back to medieval times. Both flat stones and edge stones were used for all manner of things from milling or grinding oats, barley and rape to crushing ore, pulping wood for paper manufacture and sharpening knives. The quarries closed at the end of the 19th century, leaving countless abandoned millstones among the debris.

🏠 Longshaw

The Duke of Rutland acquired Longshaw in the 1820s as a grouse shoot, building an impressive lodge to accommodate his sporting guests. The immediate surroundings were laid out with gardens and walks, with a carriage drive leading into the upper valley. On the 8th Duke's death, Sheffield Corporation wanted the land, but a campaign by Sheffield Ramblers secured it for the National Trust in 1928. Later converted to flats, the NT retains a café, shop and the surrounding land.

☆ **Toad's Mouth**

1 mile 🏠 🏠 1½ miles 🏠

3 ► Cross to gate opposite and descend steps to a fork.
► Bear **right** to bridge over Burbage Brook.

4 ► Across it, swing **right**, upstream, eventually reaching another bridge.
► Cross and climb to junction by small waterfall.

5 ► To see Toad's Mouth, bear **left**, climbing to gate onto main road.
► Go **left** over Burbage Bridge and immediately cross to signposted step-stile, **right**. The strangely shaped rock rears to your **left**.

NATURE NOTES

Red deer are occasionally seen in the woods, while bats emerge to hunt as the day closes. There are mandarin ducks on the lake and among other bird species are redstart and spotted flycatcher. Listen out for the 'yaffle' call of green woodpeckers in the woods while the mournful call of the curlew might be heard on the moors.

Redstart

Above: curlew
Left: mandarin duck

☆ Millstone Quarries

| 2 miles

6 ➡ Return to **5**, branching **left** to carry on through wood.
➡ 50 yards beyond a gate, watch for a fainter path forking **left**.
➡ It leads to another gate onto main road.

☆ Packhorse Bridge

8

| 2½ miles

7 ➡ Cross to track opposite and follow it through a couple of gates.
➡ Stick with ongoing track across the moor for ½ mile to prominent fork.
➡ Bear **left** and head gently down for another ¼ mile to packhorse bridge.

Red deer

Above:
spotted flycatcher
Below:
green woodpecker

🏠 3 miles

9

🚌 3½ miles

P

🏠 V 🚻 ☕
Longshaw
Lodge

8 ➡ Return to main road, crossing to gated path opposite, **7**.
➡ Keep forward, branching **left** to rejoin the estate drive.
➡ Follow it **left** to large white gate at the end.

9 ➡ Cross road to another gate opposite; resume on estate drive to return to **1**.
➡ Go **left** and **left** again back to car park.

Opposite (clockwise): red deer;
conkers on a horse chestnut tree;
skylark
This page (clockwise): orange-tip
butterfly; whitethroat; Canada geese;
foxglove

MACCLESFIELD CANAL AND RAILWAY

An easy and almost entirely flat walk on the outskirts of Poynton: the first leg follows the line of a former railway, sometimes passing through deep, wooded cuttings and elsewhere crossing brooks that ultimately end in the River Mersey; the return is along the still-busy Macclesfield Canal, which loops round the Peak foothills below Lyme Park.

Distance	2.8 miles/4.5 km
Time	1¼ hours
Start/Finish	Nelson Pit car park, near Higher Poynton
Parking	SK12 1TH Nelson Pit car park
Public toilets	Beside information centre in car park
Cafés/pubs	Boars Head, Original Coffee Tavern near start; The Miner's Arms, Adlington
Terrain	Former railway line and canal towpath
Hilliness	Largely flat but with gentle rise to ④
Footwear	Year round 🥾

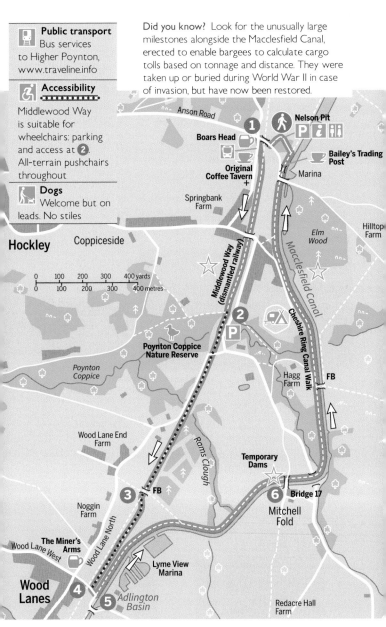

Public transport
Bus services
to Higher Poynton,
www.traveline.info

Accessibility
Middlewood Way
is suitable for
wheelchairs: parking
and access at ❷.
All-terrain pushchairs
throughout

Dogs
Welcome but on
leads. No stiles

Did you know? Look for the unusually large
milestones alongside the Macclesfield Canal,
erected to enable bargees to calculate cargo
tolls based on tonnage and distance. They were
taken up or buried during World War II in case
of invasion, but have now been restored.

Anson Road

Nelson Pit

Boars Head

Bailey's Trading
Post

Original
Coffee Tavern

Marina

Springbank
Farm

Elm
Wood

Hilltop
Farm

Hockley   Coppiceside

0   100   200   300   400 yards
0   100   200   300   400 metres

Middlewood Way
(dismantled railway)

Macclesfield Canal

Cheshire Ring Canal Walk

Poynton Coppice
Nature Reserve

Poynton
Coppice

Hagg
Farm

FB

Wood Lane End
Farm

Rams Clough

Temporary
Dams

Bridge 17

Mitchell
Fold

Noggin
Farm

FB

The Miner's
Arms
Wood Lane West

Wood Lane North

Lyme View
Marina

**Wood
Lanes**

Adlington
Basin

Redacre Hall
Farm

STORIES BEHIND THE WALK

☆ A Branch Line

Initially opened in 1869 as a single track providing a passenger service between Macclesfield and Marple, the line was soon carrying goods and upgraded to double track. A link, immediately north of Poynton Station, connected it to the network of mineral lines serving the main pits of the local coalfield and generated considerable traffic until the mines closed in 1935. The line remained open for another 35 years before becoming a victim of the Beeching Review but subsequently found new life as the Middlewood Way and a linear park.

☆ Poynton's Mines

Nelson Pit was one of about 70 coal mines around Poynton. Surface outcrops and shallow bell pits had been worked since at least the middle of the 16th century, but as water and then steam replaced manpower and horse gins to raise the coal, deeper seams could be worked. The coal at Nelson Pit was some 133 yards below ground. At the industry's peak in the mid-19th century, the area produced around 250,000 tons of coal a year.

Poynton Coppice Nature Reserve

1½ mile

Boars Head
Original Coffee Tavern

☆ Old Railway Middlewood Way

➡ Turn **right** out of car park entrance along Lyme Road.
➡ Over bridge reach crossroads opposite The Boars Head (with The Original Coffee Tavern, left).

1 ➡ Immediately turn sharp **left** through gate leading to Middlewood Way.
➡ Path slopes down to former station. Carry on to Poynton Coppice.

☆ Temporary Dams

Stop planks, such as those seen beside bridge 17, are a common feature along the waterway network and can be fitted into slots cut into the bank stonework to form a temporary dam. This enables sections of the canal to be drained for maintenance and they are an emergency resource should the canal bank burst. The most disastrous such incident on the Macclesfield Canal was a breach at Kerridge in February 1912, when the embankment gave way, draining the whole canal as far as the top lock at Bosley and causing widespread damage.

☆ Macclesfield Canal

Railways were already beginning to out-compete canals when the 26-mile Macclesfield Canal opened in 1831, and indeed, the waterway was bought out in 1846. Nevertheless, it continued as a commercial waterway, its main cargoes being coal, cotton, stone and a fast-packet passenger service. Commercial traffic finally came to an end in 1954, but by then the North Cheshire Cruising Club, Britain's earliest such organisation, was already firmly established on the canal, thus ensuring it was never closed.

1 mile

☆ O l d   R a i l w a y
M i d d l e w o o d   W a y

The Miner's Arms (right)

Adlington Basin

2 ▬ Poynton Coppice Nature Reserve (right) offers an optional short circular trail.
▬ Continue along old railway, eventually reaching a high bridge across cutting.

3 ▬ Immediately beyond bridge, take the parallel footpath **left**.
▬ This rises to run along top of the wooded embankment. It ends through a kissing-gate onto lane beside Lyme Breeze.

NATURE NOTES

Poynton Coppice is one of only a handful of working coppices in the county, producing small wood for hurdles, fencing and firewood. Among the trees are oak, ash, hazel, elm, alder, birch, holly and sycamore. Areas of the wood are coppiced in cycles of around 12 years. Alder was used by a local clog maker.

Coppicing opens the understorey to sunlight, encouraging flowers such as bluebells and also bramble, which provides cover for small birds such as wrens. Butterflies include the speckled wood and the rare white-letter hairstreak whose caterpillars feed on elm, while heron can sometimes be spotted along the canal bank.

Above: heron
Left: coppicing

☆ Temporary Dams

1½ miles   Bridge 17   2 miles

☆ **M a c c l e s f i e l d   C a n a l**

4 ➤ Turn **left** up towards bridge over Macclesfield Canal.
➤ Just before bridge, leave through kissing-gate on left onto canal towpath.

5 ➤ Walk away from the bridge past Adlington Basin, a former colliery wharf.
➤ After ¾ mile, pass beneath bridge 17.

Bluebells

Oak tree

Alder

☆ Macclesfield Canal

2½ miles   Bailey's
Trading Post

P
🚻
ℹ️

6 ➧ It is then only 1 mile further along towpath back to Nelson Pit.
➧ After crossing a bridge over boatyard inlet and Bailey's Trading Post, turn **left** back into car park.

Blackberries, fruit of the bramble

TEGG'S NOSE

Tegg's Nose is an impressive feature when viewed from below. Tackled from the country park though, it is an easy path onto the hill which spectacularly overlooks the Cheshire Plain to the Welsh hills. The trail leads past former quarries and some of the old machinery that was once used there to the viewpoint. There is then a long but simple descent to a couple of reservoirs above Langley, and then an inevitable but straightforward climb back to complete the circuit.

Distance	2.7 miles/4.3km
Time	1¾ hours
Start/Finish	Tegg's Nose Country Park
Parking	SK11 0AP Tegg's Nose Country Park car park
Public toilets	At start, in country park visitor centre
Cafés/pubs	Café at start, in visitor centre; pub in Langley, just off route
Terrain	Surfaced tracks, hillside and woodland paths
Hilliness	Steep descent off Tegg's Nose ❸ to ❹ with steady climb back to car park from ❼

Did you know? Tegg's Nose is one of the
highpoints along the Gritstone Trail, Cheshire's
35-mile long-distance footpath, which climbs
over the hill as it traces the line of the county's
gritstone outcrops and scarps at the edge of the
vast Cheshire Plain between Kidsgrove and Disley.

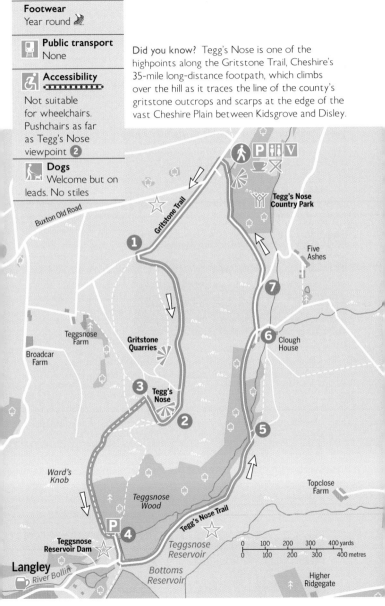

STORIES BEHIND THE WALK

☆ Reservoirs

Bottoms Reservoir was constructed in 1850, the first of several waterbodies to regulate the water supply powering the mills in Langley and further downstream. Teggsnose and Ridgegate followed 20 years later with Trentabank being built in the 1920s, the latter two to provide drinking water for the rapidly expanding towns. Much of the surrounding conifer plantation was established shortly after to filter groundwater and reduce pollution in the catchment area.

☆ Silk

Macclesfield's silk industry began in the 14th century with the manufacture of fashionable buttons, but soon expanded to weaving, printing and dying silk fabric. The fast-flowing streams of the River Bollin headwaters provided power to turn the mills, while the copious supply of pure water was necessary for the production process. At one time there were five mills established below Tegg's Nose in Langley, one of which still produces fine silk fabric today.

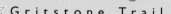

Tegg's Nose Country Park — 1 — Gritstone Quarries

½ mile

☆ Gritstone Trail

➡ Leaving car park entrance, turn **left** along laneside pathway: Gritstone Trail.

➡ Keep to trail as lane then bends away right.

➡ Pass through a gate/kissing-gate and continue to a second.

1 ➡ Take either the steps immediately up **left** (or walk briefly **forward** and then swing **left**).

➡ The paths combine to lead past old workings/machinery.

➡ Carry on above a deep quarry pit to the tip of Tegg's Nose.

☀ Gritstone Quarries

Stone has been quarried from the hill since at least the 16th century, exploiting separate outcrops on the top of the hill and where the car park and information centre now stand. The thinly bedded gritstone could be sharply cut and was valued for use both as building stone and for flags, kerbs and cobbles. It was apparently exported as far away as the Isle of Man, while closer to home it paved the streets of Macclesfield.

☀ A Royal Hunting Forest

To the south-east, Tegg's Nose looks out over the woodland plantations of Macclesfield Forest, a small remnant of a royal hunting forest under the control of the Earls of Chester. It stretched between the Goyt and Dane valleys and onto the moorland foothills of the Peak. Much of the present forest consists of commercially planted conifer, but there are areas of semi-natural woodland too. Although the wild boar and wolves of Norman England have long gone, deer still roam here.

☀ Tegg's Nose

2 ☀ 3 | 1 mile

2 ➡ The trail sweeps **right** above a steep slope of quarry waste.
➡ Ignore gate opposite stone bench and continue another 100 yards to find a second gate on **left**.

3 ➡ Through it, the Gritstone Trail drops down steps; keep ahead over sloping grass.
➡ Beyond, trail continues steadily down; later, use kissing-gate into woodland.
➡ Beyond a second kissing-gate, descend steps and wind out into car park at bottom.

NATURE NOTES

The stark snout of Tegg's Nose is covered in stone waste from the quarries and is sparsely covered with heather, gorse, crowberry and bilberry.

Holly, whose wood was used in the manufacture of buttons, is a feature of Teggsnose Wood, while grassland plants such as harebell, mountain pansy, tormentil and common spotted orchid may be seen in flower on the open meadow areas.

Listen out for the 'cronk' call of the raven and in woodland you might spot a nuthatch. Tufted duck can be seen on the open waters of the reservoirs, while Trentabank Reservoir (visible from the summit of Tegg's Nose) claims to have the largest heronry in the Peak District.

Top: harebell
Above: gorse
Left: tufted duck

Teggsnose Reservoir Dam
To Langley (right)

1½ miles   2 miles

4 ➡ Follow track **right** across Teggsnose Reservoir dam.
➡ At far side, turn **left** along rough track, signed Tegg's Nose Trail.
➡ Keep with it past the reservoir, eventually dipping to ford a stream.

5 ➡ The track resumes its steady climb, eventually emerging onto the bend of a lane.

Holly

Top: bilberry
Above: crowberry

Tegg's Nose
Country Park

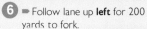

2½ miles

6 ➤ Follow lane up **left** for 200 yards to fork.

7 ➤ Branch off **left** onto a sett-paved track, which climbs back to the car park.

MONSAL TRAIL AND CHEE DALE

The full walk follows the Monsal Trail along the course of an abandoned railway, engineered via tunnels and viaducts along the narrow, twisting Chee Dale gorge. The return is along a pretty riverside path that involves stepping stones and some clambering. The most awkward sections can be avoided by climbing back to the Monsal Trail at **7**, although the final stretch by the river from **8** follows a good path and is not to be missed.

Distance	4.3 miles/6.9km
Time	2½ hours
Start/Finish	Millers Dale
Parking SK17 8SN	Millers Dale car park, off B6049
Public toilets	In car park at start
Cafés/pubs	Café in car park at start; Angler's Rest pub in Millers Dale village
Terrain	Broad track along Monsal Trail; occasionally rough riverside path with two stretches of stepping stones
Hilliness	Mostly level, but some clambering over rocks

Footwear
Monsal Trail:
Year round 👟
Riverside path:
Year round 🥾

📷 **Public transport**
Bus services to
Millers Dale, www.
traveline.info

♿ **Accessibility**
Wheelchairs and
pushchairs along
Monsal Trail to ❹

🐕 **Dogs**
Welcome but on
leads. One stile; two
stretches of stepping
stones

Did you know? With two viaducts, five
platforms, sidings, goods sheds, a cattle dock and
even a post office, Millers Dale was once one of
the largest stations on the Midland Railway's
London to Manchester line, with 43 departures
every day.

Local legend Stepping stones usually take you
across a river, but here in Chee Dale, they take
the path along the narrowest stretches of the
gorge. Sturdy and well-placed, they are unlikely
to be washed away, but when the water rises
they become impassable and you must return
to the Monsal Trail above.

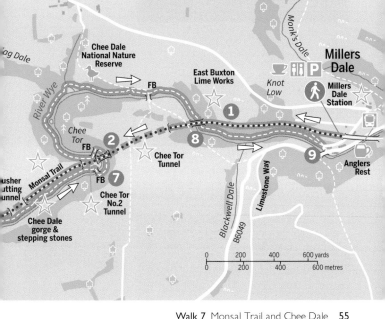

STORIES BEHIND THE WALK

☆ **The Monsal Trail** Opened as an 8½-mile leisure trail in 1981, the Monsal Trail follows the route of a disused railway between Blackwell Mill and Bakewell, passing through some exhilarating scenery. Of the six tunnels, three lie on this short section as well as several impressive viaducts, a considerable feat of engineering to take the railway through the otherwise impassable narrow, twisting gorge of Chee Dale.

☆ **The Midland Railway**
The line became part of the Midland Railway's main express route between London and Manchester, with Millers Dale Station allowing passengers to transfer onto local trains for Buxton, which had developed as a busy spa resort. Passengers for Buxton usually had to change trains, but mindful of disabled people travelling for treatment, coaches were sometimes detached from the express to be re-coupled onto the local train.

☆ **Millers Dale Station** ☆ **East Buxton Lime Works** ❶ ☆ **Chee Tor Tunnel** ❷ ☆ **Chee Tor 2 Tunnel**

1½ mile | 1 mile

☆ Monsal Trail

🅿 🏬 ☕
➤ From old station platform follow Monsal Trail to **right**.
➤ Shortly, a path off right offers a diversion to top of East Buxton Lime Works; the kilns themselves rear up beside main trail in ⅓ mile.

❶
➤ Carry on to a viaduct (where you can drop right to return on riverside path from ❽).
➤ The main walk carries on **ahead** through the long Chee Tor Tunnel.

❷
➤ Emerging at far end, cross a small viaduct into Chee Tor No. 2 Tunnel.
➤ Continue high above river for more than ½ mile, through Rusher Cutting Tunnel and over another viaduct to fork.

☆ Industry

The arrival of the railways brought massive industry to this once quiet corner of the Derbyshire Dales, with the opening of two large quarries at Millers Dale and around a dozen more beside the track towards Buxton and through Great Rock Dale. At East Buxton Lime Works, two massive kilns were cut out of the cliff beside the track, in which the stone was burnt to produce quicklime and then loaded directly onto railway wagons. Opened in 1863, the line operated for just over 100 years although much of the traffic was lost after the Millers Dale quarries closed in 1944.

☆ Little and Large

In contrast to Millers Dale, which at its height became the largest station on the Midland's London to Manchester line, Blackwell Mill (near ④) was said to be the smallest on the whole UK network. Built only to serve the railway cottages that still stand by the river, its platform was barely long enough to fit a single coach.

Look for a disused hydraulic ram beside the path after ⑧. It pumped water from the river to a large storage tank just outside the station to supply the thirsty steam engines.

☆ Rusher Cutting Tunnel — ③ — ④ — ⑤ Blackwell Mill Tuck Shop — 2 miles

1½ miles

☆ Monsal Trail

③
➡ Stay **left** below high cliffs towards Wyedale.
➡ At end of a deep cutting, pass beneath bridge to signed junction.

④
➡ Through gate on **right**, walk down past Blackwell Mill Tuck Shop and over bridge spanning River Wye to another junction by terrace of former railway cottages.

⑤
➡ Take path **right** to Chee Dale. At fork by Pennine Bridleway post (PBW), keep **right** by river.
➡ Walk on, pass a footbridge and drop beneath a viaduct to continue along the valley, shortly reaching a stile below another viaduct.

NATURE NOTES

Forget-me-not, ground elder, wild strawberry, red campion, and wintergreen are to be found along woodland verges, while grassland plants including cowslip, early purple orchid, harebell, knapweed, rockrose, ox-eye daisy, kidney vetch, bird's-foot trefoil, thyme, marjoram and bee orchid find a home in the poor soil of the abandoned quarries.

Woodland mammals include Natterer's, brown long-eared and Daubenton's bats. There are also water voles down by the river – look for a woodland carving of this timid creature. Birds include jackdaw nesting in the cliffs, and other inhabitants include swift, kestrel, garden warbler, redstart, blackbird, and whitethroat.

Water vole

Left: forget-me-nots
Right: cowslips

☆ Chee Dale gorge and stepping stones

Chee Dale National Nature Reserve

6 ⌇ 2½ miles 7 ⌇ 3 miles

Riverside Path

6 ➤ Steps up left offer an escape to Monsal Trail; otherwise keep **ahead** into narrowing gorge to progress over stepping stones.
➤ Reaching a bridge, cross to opposite bank and climb to fork.

7 ➤ The path off right climbs to Monsal Trail, while that **ahead** returns to river.
➤ Pass beneath viaduct and over bridge to north bank.
➤ Downstream, beyond more stepping stones, the rugged path leads to a final viaduct.

Kestrel

Above: early
purple orchid
Below: swifts

Jackdaw

Millers Dale
Station ☆

3½ miles   ⑧   4 miles   ⑨

8 ▸ Now on a good path,
continue downstream beside
river.
▸ Approaching Millers Dale,
emerge at a stile beside road
bridge.

9 ▸ Go sharp **left** up stepped
path back to Monsal Trail.
▸ At the top, turn **right** to
car park.

Walk 7 Monsal Trail and Chee Dale   **59**

Opposite (clockwise):
The Fleece Inn,
Holme; The Castle,
Castleton.
This page (clockwise):
Boars Head, Poynton;
Three Roofs,
Castleton; Stableyard
Grab and Go, Ilam;
Original Coffee
Tavern, Poynton;
Bank View Café,
Langsett

BUXTON
COUNTRY PARK

Climbing a wooded hillside to the south of the town, Buxton Country Park has everything for an exciting family day out. Local wildlife might be glimpsed from winding woodland paths, while the open meadows above are renowned for their carpets of colourful wildflowers in spring and summer. At the top of the hill, a Victorian folly offers fine views over the town, while back at the start you can explore the subterranean passages of Poole's Cavern.

Distance	1.4 miles / 2.3km
Time	1 hour
Start / Finish	Poole's Cavern, Buxton
Parking SK17 9BB	Poole's Cavern car park, Green Lane
Public toilets	At start
Cafés / pubs	Café at the Cavern, at start
Terrain	Woodland and rough, grassy hillside paths
Hilliness	Undulating paths throughout
Footwear	Winter Spring/Autumn Summer

Did you know? At around 1,100 feet above sea level, Buxton is England's highest market town, so you might wonder why the hill above it is called 'Grin Low' and not, perhaps, 'Grin High'. 'Low' here derives from *hlaw*, an Old English word meaning hill or barrow, and appears in many of the Peak District's hill names.

Local legend Solomon's Temple was originally built around 1835 as a make-work scheme funded by the Duke of Devonshire to help alleviate local unemployment. Its name remembers Solomon Mycock, one-time landlord of the Cheshire Cheese and who leased the hill for grazing. However, constructed of drystone, the tower eventually fell down and was rebuilt in 1894 by public subscription. It stands on the site of a barrow, the excavation of which revealed Bronze Age burials and cremations as well as Roman artefacts.

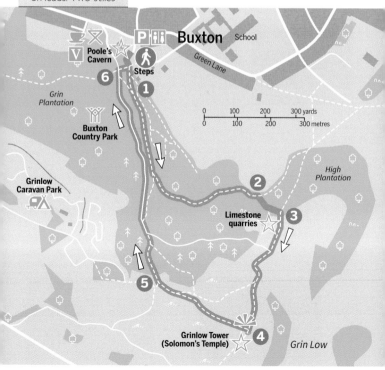

STORIES BEHIND
THE WALK

☆ **Limestone Quarries** The hillside is littered with quarry workings dating back to the 16th century, the limestone being burnt to produce quicklime for fertiliser, mortar and iron smelting. But by the 19th century, as Buxton developed into a fashionable spa resort, the unsightly workings drew complaints from the visiting elite. In response, to hide the eyesore, the Duke of Devonshire planted the lower slopes with trees, which, over time, have become a haven for local wildlife.

☆ **Buxton's Origins** To the Celts, warm water gushing from the ground was the sacred gift of a goddess, who the Romans later adopted as their own. They built a temple and bathhouse and called it Aquae Arnemetiae. The waters' curative reputation has persisted through the centuries and Mary, Queen of Scots, regularly visited during her long captivity in Derbyshire.

 ☆ Poole's Cavern

 🏃 Steps ① ¼ mile

🏕 Buxton Country Park

 P

 🚻

 V

 ☕ ✕

➡ From the pay machine by the visitor centre, follow raised path round the car park to steps at foot of the wood.
➡ At the top bear **left** in front of large, wooden mural along a rising path, passing a carved hedgehog to junction.

① ➡ Follow the path **left**, with more representations of woodland animals and plants.
➡ At a fork, keep **left** past carvings of a seed pod and then a cute mouse, sticking with the main path to another fork by a carved hare.

☆ Attractions for a Georgian Spa Town

Buxton developed as a grand Georgian spa under the 5th Duke of Devonshire, who invested profits from his Ecton copper mines to create a grand resort. An elegant crescent, emulating that at Bath, hotels, a pump room, ballroom and assembly rooms attracted the rich and famous to 'take the waters'. Parks and gardens were established and Poole's Cavern became a formal attraction, the entrance being opened up and the chambers furnished with candelabra to illuminate the wondrous formations.

☆ **Poole's Cavern** Early visitors to this spectacular cave included Daniel Defoe, and Charles Cotton who named it one of his 'Seven Wonders of the Peak'. Visitors had to crawl in on all fours. Disreputable guides might abandon them to the dark unless they dug deeper into their pockets for a tip.

☆ Limestone Quarries

½ mile

3 ➡ Turn through gate onto open hillside.
➡ Head uphill beside broken wall; pass a dew pond and then a large mound, aiming for Solomon's Temple, which peeps into view.
➡ Over a stile in a crossing wall higher up, carry on to tower on top of hill.

2 ➡ Branch **right** and climb to junction at the top by gate.

NATURE NOTES

The wood, managed for the benefit of wildlife, includes over a dozen different types of tree: ash, elm, beech and sycamore predominate, but look out for rowan, hawthorn and horse chestnut – the conker tree.

The trees attract many birds, some of which are common in gardens such as song thrush, great tit, blue tit and chaffinch. But look out too for more unusual species such as great spotted woodpecker, pied flycatcher, treecreeper or even tawny owl.

Small rodents such as the wood mouse scurry about in the leaf litter and grey squirrel bound along branches. Fox and badger are harder to spot, but they live there as well.

Top left: treecreeper
Left: grey squirrel
Right: wood mouse

☆ Solomon's
❋ Temple

④————————————⑤————————┆

┆ ¾ mile   1 mile ┆

④ ▸ Turn **right** in front of tower (left as you come out if you've been inside) and pick your way across a grassy moonscape towards a pair of redundant stone gateposts in the middle distance.
▸ Bear **right** to a wall stile leading back into wood.

Top right: great spotted woodpecker
Top left: horse chestnut flowers
Left: fox

Buxton Country Park ⍦

Poole's Cavern ☆

1¼ miles

6 Steps

5 ▸ Follow signs to Poole's Cavern and Buxton along downhill track where wayside sculptures represent limestone fossils.
▸ Beyond the sculpture of a miner, a path joins from the right.

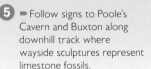

6 ▸ To avoid a stepped descent, double back **right** on lower path to 1 and there go sharp **left**.
▸ Otherwise, continue a little further forward and then turn **right** down flight of steps back to car park.

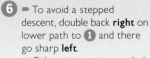

Walk 8 Buxton Country Park **67**

MANIFOLD WAY

Winding for a little over 8 miles along the picturesque river valleys of the Manifold and Hamps, the Manifold Way is one of the most user-friendly leisure paths in the whole of the Peak District. Following the almost-level course of a former railway through narrow, twisting valleys, it swaps scenes of the wooded river for more distant views to the surrounding hills. This section of the trail loops back along a quiet lane, but those wanting a longer walk can simply continue further along the valley to Wetton Mill, where there is a café.

Distance	3.2 miles/5.2 km
Time	1¾ hours
Start/Finish	Hulme End National Park Centre
Parking SK17 0HF	National Park car park at start
Public toilets	National Park visitor centre at start
Cafés/pubs	Tea Junction café at start; Manifold Inn, Hulme End village
Terrain	Tracks and lanes; short section of field path
Hilliness	Level throughout
Footwear	Year round

Did you know? The name of the Manifold Valley describes it perfectly, for in its short journey through the gorge from Hulme End to the river's confluence with the River Dove below Ilam, it squirms this way and that countless times.

Did you know? A man 'wi' no yed' is said to gallop on a white horse through the Manifold Valley on moonlit nights – so, watch out if you are about after dark!

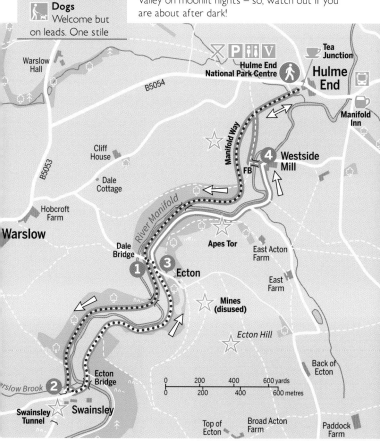

STORIES BEHIND THE WALK

☆ **Ecton Mines** Copper has been mined at Ecton for perhaps 4,000 years, peaking during the late 18th century, when it was the richest and deepest copper mine in the world. The massive hill above the lane is riddled with tunnels and shafts descending more than 1,000 feet below the level of the river. The striking building seen on top of the hill housed a steam-driven winding engine and there was even an underground canal constructed to transport the ore from the working seams.

Hulme End National Park Centre

☆ **Hulme End** For much of its history, the hilly countryside of the Peak was more suited to packhorse than cart for the long-distance transport of goods. The arrival of the turnpike at Hulme End around 1780, brought with it a certain prosperity with a new bridge across the river, a toll house and a coaching inn, which began life as the Jolly Carter and is now the Manifold Inn.

½ mile

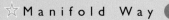

☆ **Manifold Way** ❶

➡ Follow signed Manifold Trail away from car park for ¾ mile, crossing a bridge over river and eventually meeting a lane at Ecton.

➡ Cross lane and continue with ongoing trail opposite.
➡ The track crosses river once more and, after passing through a gate and small parking area, emerges onto lane opposite Swainsley Tunnel.

☆ Apes Tor

At Apes Tor there were several small quarries alongside the lane, and the exposed cliffs show superb examples of the way the limestone strata have been faulted and folded. Bricked and gated entrances to the old mines can be seen, and old records show that a horse-powered gin was used here to lift ore to the surface from the canal, some 200 feet below ground.

☆ **Railway** Built in 1904, primarily to serve a large creamery at Ecton, the Leek and Manifold Valley Light Railway's two engines chugged up and down this quiet valley for 30 years, taking milk down to the main line for onward dispatch to London. Standard-gauge freight wagons and tankers were carried on special dollies so that milk could be quickly transferred to the main line at Waterhouses, and during busy holiday weekends, goods wagons were fitted with plank seats to accommodate extra passengers.

> 1 mile · · · Swainsley Tunnel · · · 1½ miles · Ecton Bridge

☆ M a n i f o l d   W a y

2 ➡ Turn **left** down lane to junction and go **left** again, signed Hulme End.
➡ Cross a bridge over river; the way curves below Ecton Hill, passing old quarry workings before reaching junction close to **1**.
➡ To avoid field path section from **1**, turn left then right through gate to return along Manifold Way.

NATURE NOTES

The River Manifold, where it runs above ground, is home to several species of fish, including trout, European bullhead and lamprey eels. Although native crayfish were largely decimated by disease in 2008, there are hopes for their return. Occasional sightings of otter have been reported.

The flowing water attracts kingfisher and dipper as well as dragonfly species and mayfly. Flowering plants include butterbur, bluebell, foxglove, ramson, water avens, and lords and ladies, while old walls and adjacent meadows make an ideal habitat for weasel and stoat.

Above: butterbur
Right: lamprey eel
Opposite: kingfisher, lords and ladies, dipper

Ecton Hill and Mines
(high above lane)

2 miles

3 ➡ Remain on lane past junction, still signed to Hulme End.
➡ Pass the striking rock face at Apes Tor, where a gated adit opens onto a shaft above an underground canal that served the Ecton copper mines.
➡ Walk on, ignoring lane off to Back of Ecton and shortly reaching Westside Mill.

Weasel

Hulme End National
Park Centre

Apes Tor

2½ miles

4 Westside Mill

3 miles

4 ➡ Immediately past its barn,
turn **left** along contained path
to cross bridge over River
Manifold.

➡ Bear **right** across
rough pasture to gate,
continuing the line beyond to
second gate.

➡ Emerging back onto
Manifold Trail, go **right**, back
to Hulme End.

ILAM

One of the prettiest in Derbyshire, the 19th-century estate village of Ilam offers an enjoyable and relaxing stroll taking in parkland, woods and riverside. There's plenty to see along the way including the resurgences of underground rivers, a Saxon cross and an interesting church that has Saxon roots. Although the village has no pub, there is a National Trust tearoom in Ilam Hall.

Distance	1.9 miles/3km
Time	1 hour
Start/Finish	Ilam Hall
Parking DE6 2AZ	National Trust car park
Public toilets	Ilam Hall
Cafés/pubs	National Trust tearoom
Terrain	Lanes, tracks and open grassy hillside
Hilliness	Gently undulating

Footwear
Winter
Spring/Autumn
Summer

Public transport
None

Accessibility

Wheelchair access is limited to the immediate surroundings of Ilam Hall. All-terrain pushchairs throughout with care, except after prolonged wet weather

Dogs
Welcome but on leads. One stile

Did you know? Ilam Hall had already been partly demolished in the 1930s when it was bought by Sir Robert McDougall, of the famous flour-milling family, who restored what was left and gifted it to the National Trust for use as a youth hostel.

Local legend Buried in Ilam church are the remains of St Bertram, an 8th-century Mercian prince who turned hermit after a wolf killed his wife and child. Heartbroken, he renounced his birthright for a life of prayer and solitude in a nearby cave. Once, when hungry and tempted by the Devil to turn stones into bread, he instead prayed for bread to be turned into stones.

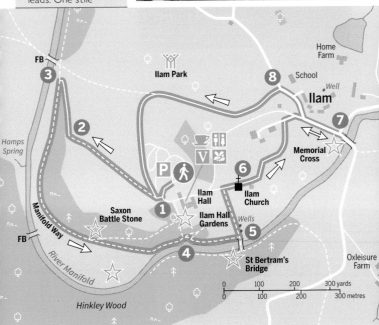

STORIES BEHIND THE WALK

Ilam's History Originally a Saxon village, Ilam became part of the estates of Burton Abbey in the 11th century, when it was refounded as a Benedictine House. A small monastic settlement managed the estate, which, after the Dissolution in 1541, was bought by the influential Port family. They built a Tudor mansion overlooking the river and lived there for 250 years. At the beginning of the 19th century, the estate was bought by David Pike Watts, a wealthy London vintner, to whom there is a memorial in the church.

A Country Estate

In 1816, the estate passed to Mary, Watts' daughter, who by then had married the wealthy Jesse Russell. Incorporating his wife's name, Watts-Russell replaced the old hall with a massive new mansion and remodelled the village in a 'Swiss Alpine' style. The estate eventually passed to his eldest son and then to Robert Hanbury who, among other improvements, planted many trees and installed hydro-generators to supply electricity to the house, farm and village.

 Ilam Hall Gardens **Ilam Park**

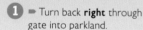

¼ mile

➤ Head towards the hall to leave bottom right corner of car park past information panel to junction at foot of steps up to The Oaks.

1 ➤ Turn back **right** through gate into parkland.
➤ With back to gate, aim directly across park to far side (350 yards; path non-existent at first) angling **left** away from fence.

☆ Disappearing Rivers

Rising respectively on the edge of Axe Moor and the flanks of Merrytown Low, the convoluted valleys of the rivers Manifold and Hamps come together below Beeston Tor. However, following prolonged dry spells, both rivers disappear below ground. Their subterranean journeys continue for several miles before resurfacing at separate boil holes by Ilam Hall. The combined river then continues its journey to meet the River Dove at the foot of Dovedale.

☆ Memorial Cross

Built to resemble an Eleanor Cross, the monument in the centre of the village was erected in 1840 by Jesse Watts-Russell as a memorial to his first wife, Mary. The original Eleanor crosses, of which there were 12, were erected at the behest of Edward I in memory of his beloved wife Eleanor of Castille, who died at Harby in 1290. These elaborately carved crosses marked the nightly resting places of the funeral cortège as her body was taken to Westminster Abbey for burial.

Saxon Battle
☆ Stone   ☆ River Manifold

| ½ mile | ¾ mile | St Bertram's Bridge |

2 ➤ Appproaching wooded bank, a field track develops that swings **right**, descending beside fence.
➤ At the bottom, it meets another track above river, often dry here (look from the bridge just ahead).

3 ➤ Double back sharp **left** through a gate.
➤ Keep with main path at foot of wooded bank.
➤ Beyond the Saxon Battle Stone, ignore consecutive paths (left) to gardens.

NATURE NOTES

Ilam Hall's gardens are well worth visiting. Prominent medieval ridge and furrow marks can be seen across the wooded park, where sheep graze freely.

The parkland includes a line of lime trees, Lebanese cedar and a giant sequoia, planted around 200 years ago.

On the lawns, pied wagtail may be seen catching flying insects, while their close cousins grey and yellow wagtail may be seen along the river bed, and buzzard soar high above the parkland.

Lime tree
Left: Ilam Park

✝ ■ Ilam Church ⑥   ☆ Memorial Cross ⑦

1 mile   1¼ miles

4 ➠ Keep **ahead** beside the now gushing river (it emerges just upstream in woods opposite).

➠ Walking by low cliff, look down to see River Manifold 'boil up' from the bank.

➠ The way then forks. Stay beside river to St Bertram's Bridge.

5 ➠ At bridge swing **left** towards church, passing walled enclosure of another spring.

➠ Turn **right** into graveyard and walk past church to gate at the far corner.

6 ➠ Follow ongoing path to Ilam Moor Road and turn **right** to reach Ilam Cross.

Buzzard

Above: yellow wagtail
Below: red campion

Ⓜ Ilam Park   Ilam Hall Gardens 🌿

m School ¦1½ miles   ¦1¾ miles

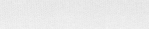

7 ➡ Retrace steps towards hall, but in front of entrance, bend **right** with lane.
➡ Walk up to the school where, opposite, a footpath is signed through gate on **left**.

8 ➡ A track leads away, winding first **right** and then **left** across the park.
➡ Passing car park, the track leads back to the gate **1**, where tearoom/gardens lie ahead.

Walk 10 Ilam   **79**

Publishing information

© Crown copyright 2022.
All rights reserved.

Ordnance Survey, OS, and the OS logos are registered trademarks, and OS Short Walks Made Easy is a trademark of Ordnance Survey Ltd.

© Crown copyright and database rights (2022) Ordnance Survey.

ISBN 978 0 319092 31 6
1st edition published by Ordnance Survey 2022.

www.ordnancesurvey.co.uk

While every care has been taken to ensure the accuracy of the route directions, the publishers cannot accept responsibility for errors or omissions, or for changes in details given. The countryside is not static: hedges and fences can be removed, stiles can be replaced by gates, field boundaries can alter, footpaths can be rerouted and changes in ownership can result in the closure or diversion of some concessionary paths. Also, paths that are easy and pleasant for walking in fine conditions may become slippery, muddy and difficult in wet weather.

If you find an inaccuracy in either the text or maps, please contact Ordnance Survey at os.uk/contact.

A catalogue record for this book is available from the British Library.

Milestone Publishing credits

Authors: Dennis and Jan Kelsall

Series editor: Kevin Freeborn

Maps: Cosmographics

Design and Production: Patrick Dawson, Milestone Publishing

Printed in Malta by Gutenberg Press

MIX
Paper from responsible sources
FSC® C022612

Photography credits

Front cover: eye35.pix / Alamy Stock Photo. **Back cover** cornfield/Shutterstock.com.

All photographs supplied by the authors ©Dennis and Jan Kelsall except pages 6 Gemma Thorpe/Ordnance Survey; 47, 78 Vivienne Crow.

The following images were supplied by Shutterstock.com: page 1, 3, 20, 21 Tom Curtis; 6 Nathan Bunseedhun; 8 Alex Manders; 10 Stanth; 18 LABETAA Andre; 18 RudiErnst; 19 Edwin Godinho; 19 Richard Fitzer; 24 Coatesy; 25 Marc Freebrey; 25 Menno Schaefer; 32 arousa; 32 Martin Fowler; 33 Duncan Andison; 33 jph9362; 33 Margo Photography; 38, 66, 73 Rudmer Zwerver; 38 Keneva Photography; 38 Zeno Swijtink; 39 Mark Bridger; 39 Petr Simon; 39 Ujhelyi; 40 SaskiaAcht; 40 Tony North; 40 Yuriy Balagula; 41 Dennis W Donohue; 41 Grigorii Pisotsckii; 41 Vlad Sokolovsky; 41 Whiteaster; 46 ClimbWhenReady; 46 MR JAMES WOODHEAD; 47 alan payne; 47 Lucy M Ryan; 52 imageBROKER.com; 52 Simonas Minkevicius; 52 Tikta Alik; 53 Nata Naumovec; 53 nnattalli; 58 claire norman; 58 Sanuta; 58 Tom Meaker; 59 Andrew Fletcher; 59 Justas in the wilderness; 59 Luka Hercigonja; 59 Mircea Costina; 60 RMC42; 64 R3d Nemesis; 65 Steve Allen; 66 LecartPhotos; 66 Nora Yero; 67 DmyTo; 67 Kirsty Cussens; 67 Sandra Standbridge; 72 Rostislav Stefanek; 73 Maren Winter; 73 Stephan Morris; 73 WildMedia; 78 Anna Mente; 79 Michael Gane; 79 Szymon Bartosz.